ŁAZIENKI

ŁAZIENKI

Photographs by
KRZYSZTOF JABŁOŃSKI

Text by
MAREK KWIATKOWSKI

INTERPRESS PUBLISHERS · WARSAW

Designed by
TADEUSZ KOBYŁKA

Production editor:
EWA DROGOSZ

Copyright by Wydawnictwo Interpress
Warszawa 1995

Printed in Croatia

ISBN 83-223-2622-x

On the frontispiece: Medallion with a likeness of Stanislaus
Augustus produced by the Wedgwood Pottery
in the late eighteenth century

WARSAW ŁAZIENKI OR ROYAL ŁAZIENKI

To these two names could also be added the Marshal's Łazienki, since in the sixteenth century the estate belonged to Stanisław Herakliusz Lubomirski, Grand Marshal of the Crown. But Royal Łazienki is probably the best name, because it is linked with the person of King Stanislaus Augustus (Poniatowski), its greatest patron, who filled it with architecture and laid out the park. In other words, he gave Łazienki the form that has remained in place to the present day. It is to him that Warsaw, and Poland, owe this residence in a landscaped park, which is outstanding as a work of art and also has incomparable, romantic charm.

When speaking of the history of Łazienki, we should however go far back into the past, to the Middle Ages, and begin its story with the stronghold of the princes of Mazovia that was situated on the edge of the sandy Vistula escarpment. This stronghold lay within today's Łazienki, near to the present Old Orangery, although some suggest other sites, for example, the area of the Botanical Gardens or somewhere near where the Ujazdów Castle now stands. But the Łazienki Park is the most probable site, since archaeological excavations carried out a quarter of a century ago pointed to the existence of some building, even though the fortifications of the stronghold were not found. The later work involved in planting the area must have obliterated traces of this stronghold. Perhaps future investigations will precisely identify the place, which, even if it is not within the bounds of the contemporary Łazienki, will certainly be somewhere in the close vicinity.

The stronghold, which was initially called Jazdów, was a strategic fortified point, guarding against incursions from the Vistula. It was probably surrounded by an earthen bank and palisade, and must have had an extramural settlement along the route running south to Czersk and north to Zakroczym. Just think that today's Jazdów and Wiejska streets run along part of this route. The first historical information about Jazdów comes in 1262, when the stronghold was taken by the Lithuanians and Ruthenians. Let us imagine that moment. The enemy hordes crossed the flood-swollen

Vistula on rafts, observed fearfully by the garrison and the inhabitants of the extra-mural settlement who had sought shelter in the fortress. The invaders climbed up the escarpment, encircled the stronghold and began the fight which ended in their capturing Jazdów. Prince Siemowit I died in the battle. The men who survived were executed, and the women and children taken captive. This gruesome event was the beginning of the history not only of Łazienki, but also indirectly of Warsaw. For this is the first written record of the city's past.

The rebuilt stronghold was destroyed again in 1281, this time not by an invading tribe but as a result of an internecine struggle between the Mazovian princes Conrad II and Boleslaus II. It was this second event which is supposed to have determined the moving of the court of the princes of Mazovia from Jazdów to the site of the present Royal Castle. Jazdów, which was again rebuilt and eventually changed its name to Ujazdów, became a place where the princes occasionally stayed and where court sitting and other meetings were held. The marshy, wooded terrain at the foot of the escarpment was a good place for hunting, and was later called the Animal Reserve. However we know nothing of what happened here in the fourteenth and fifteenth centuries, for the chronicles kept silent until the sixteenth century.

After the line of Mazovian princes died out in 1526, the principality became part of the Polish crown territories. King Sigismund I visited Warsaw only twice, but his wife, Bona Sforza, came here more often, since she received Mazovia as her marriage portion and from 1548 lived permanently in Ujazdów. The queen began to take over the land bordering on Ujazdów. In this way she built up a significant estate, where on the Ujazdów manor farm, she grew vegetables, thereby teaching Poles how to use them in their cuisine. Thereafter vegetables were called *włoszczyzna,* that is, coming, like Queen Bona, from Italy, or *Włochy* in Polish. A large wooden house, in fact a palace, was built at Ujazdów, which we know from the plans drawn up for it in 1606 by Alessandro Albertini. It may have been built for Queen Bona, or perhaps – and in fact this is more likely – for her daughter, Anne Jagiellon, probably in the third quarter of the sixteenth century. The building stood on the terrace of the escarpment, about two hundred metres to the north of the later Ujazdów Castle. The central part of the palace, which was almost certainly two storeys high and decorated with porches, contained reception rooms, while the residential chambers were in the wings. The traveller Giovanni Paolo Mucante, who accompanied the papal legate, Enrico Gaetani, in 1596, described the building as having "rooms covered in beautiful tapestry, with great, splendid carpets"; some chambers moreover were draped in "crimson velvet with golden fringes, just as in the papal apartments".

In 1578, the palace was the scene of the wedding ceremony of the chancellor Jan Zamoyski and Krystyna Radziwiłłówna, during which Jan Kochanowski's drama, *The Dismissal of the Greek Envoys,* was performed for the first time. On the western side, the palace was surrounded by an Italian garden, regularly laid out. At the bottom of the escarpment, down which a flight of steps led, there was a pavilion containing a bath house, probably with a spring. When the poet, Adam Jarzębski, described this residence in 1643 in his famous guide-book to Warsaw entitled *Gościniec abo opisanie Warszawy* (The highway, or a description of Warsaw), he noted, "and at the bottom a bath house with a fish pond in a hollow". Perhaps the pond that lies below the escarpment just by the Łazienkowska motorway viaduct marks the site of that earlier bath house.

At the foot of the escarpment, there were also extensive wooded places which were fenced in and where various wild animals were kept. Mucante described this as follows: "In the middle was a high garden wall, from which, without the slightest danger, we were able to observe the animals". There is no mention of hunting here. It was an animal reserve, as is apparently confirmed by the description in Jarzębski's *Gościniec*:

> *Of animals you'll find each kind,*
> *Rabbit, hare, roe deer and hind.*
> *The birds trill sweet notes high and low*
> *And fish swim deep in pools below.*
>
> *Lush meadows where the grass grows high –*
> *Gaze, you who ride the straight road by!*
> *And there behold what's not in Rome,*
> *Nor Turkey, nor Crimea's shore:*
> *Spinneys, woods, deep shrubberies,*
> *Hills, lakes, thickets and much more –*
> *Amazing views of beauty rare*
> *Impossible to find elsewhere.*
> *Should painters roam the whole world round,*
> *And seek all subjects for their art,*
> *More beauteous spot they ne'er could find*
> *To glad the eye and ease the heart.*

We can today locate this animal reserve in the region of the Piaseczyński canal, although it gave its name to the whole area at the foot of the escarpment, and the name remained in use for two centuries.

On the terrace of the escarpment, to the west of the ancient road, lay the village of Ujazdów. At the end of the village, on a promontory of the escarpment which stretches behind it, on the site of the present southern terrace of the Belvedere Palace, there was a wooden church, built on the initiative of Anne Jagiellon in 1596. This little church survived until 1818, when it was pulled down.

In 1624, King Sigismund III Vasa built a new, brick castle. It was a quadrangle with an inner courtyard and an arcaded walk on two inner sides. The corners of the building had hexagonal towers with cupolas. For appearances' sake the castle was given the outward trappings of a fortified structure, although in fact it was not so at all. The building contained, for example, a large picture gallery. The castle was splendidly situated, on a projecting promontory of the escarpment, at an angle to the line of the Vistula. This private royal residence, with its majestic, impressive appearance, was a landmark for river barges approaching Warsaw. Most probably the late Renaissance castle was built by Matteo Castelli and Constante Tencalla, the same architects who supervised the reconstruction of the Royal Castle in Warsaw. During the Polish-Swedish war of 1656-57, the castle was plundered, and thereafter for several years, the mint was located here.

Belvedere, which was built before 1663 near the above-mentioned wooden church, is inextricably linked with the history of Ujazdów, and therefore also of Łazienki. The area where Belvedere was later erected, was purchased by Krzysztof Zygmunt Pac, the Grand Chancellor of Lithuania, in 1659. Perhaps Pac's choice of site was determined by the proximity of the royal residence at Ujazdów. The name "Belvedere", which appears in a document dating from 1663, shows that Pac was aware of the attractiveness of the site that he had chosen for his residence, on the edge of the terrace of the escarpment, with wide views over the Vistula valley. Apart from its site, this first "Belvedere" had nothing in common with today's palace. It was a villa, perhaps built of timber, and square in plan. It was given by Pac to his pretty wife, Claire Isabelle de Mailly Lascaris, one of the French ladies of the bedchamber of Queen Marie Louise. No detailed plans of the building, or views of it have come down to us. We know, however, that although it was in effect a modest suburban villa, it must have been a rather impressive residence. In 1677, Courland envoys who had come to Warsaw to pay homage to the newly elected king, John III (Sobieski), stayed here. And it was also at the Belvedere in 1690 that the meeting took place between James Sobieski's fiancée, a princess of Bayern-Neuburg, and his mother, Marie Casimire. On the eastern side, there was a gradually descending garden laid out geometrically on the slope of the escarpment, with an irregular pond which is still there today.

Soon after the Belvedere was built, its surroundings began to change. The nearby Ujazdów Castle passed into the hands of Teodor Denhoff, who in 1674 ceded it to his son-in-law, Stanisław Herakliusz Lubomirski, the Grand Marshal of the Crown. The latter was not only a statesman, but also possessed of an exceptional intellect: he was erudite, a philosopher and a poet. He began his time at the Ujazdów Castle by altering its interiors, using for this purpose the services of the greatest architect working in Poland, Tylman van Gameren. Lubomirski also erected two entirely new buildings: two pavilions in the wooded area below the castle. Both have survived until today, although they have been considerably altered.

The first is the Hermitage situated in Agrykola Street near the monument to King John III. The building is square, one storey high and covered with a mansard roof. This form dates from the times of Stanislaus Augustus Poniatowski, when it was the villa of the king's mistress, Sophie Henriette Lhullier. We do not know exactly what it looked like in Lubomirski's day, apart from the fact that the walls remain the same, and that it had a multilateral annexe in the south. The interior probably contained comfortable rooms with inscriptions on the walls praising the peace that comes from solitude. And so it was the marshal's retreat. Here – like a hermit – he withdrew from the bustle of public life and gave himself up to meditation. The building was some distance from the Ujazdów Castle and hidden in a thicket.

The other pavilion that Lubomirski built, known as the Łazienka, or the bath house, did not have to be hidden amidst trees, since it served other and more joyful purposes. It was situated on an island, rectangular in shape, surrounded by the water of the canal, and it was therefore open to view. It was built on the northern edge of the island, so that part of its walls overhung the land. The base of the northern side of the building was therefore directly lapped by water. Tylman van Gameren, who designed the building, must clearly have wished to show the influence of Dutch architecture.

The water that surrounded the island was formed from a stream which flowed beneath the escarpment from south to north. Near the Bath House this irregular stream turned into a regular canal, several metres wide, which divided to encircle the island holding the pavilion. The canals on the two sides of the Palace on the Lake are what remains of this original plan. To the north, there was a rectangular artificial lake with a fountain in the centre. Unlike the case of the Hermitage, we have exact information about Lubomirski's Bath House. It was basically square, although on the northern side, there was a triangular protruding element which was the external face of an octagonal room. In the centre of the building, there was a circular room covered by a dome with a skylight in the roof. The south-facing front of the building was two storeys high in the centre and had a triangular gable. On the northern side the corners formed towers one storey high with onion domes. Both outside and inside, the building was richly decorated with stucco and wall paintings. Some elements of this décor have survived to the present day. The exterior decoration has been preserved in the central part, behind the columns of the portico which was added later. Over the main doors, there is a Latin inscription in a Baroque cartouche, strangely designed in a way that makes it difficult to decipher. You have to read it by putting together the words from the top and bottom lines in each case. It is a kind of rebus. The first verse, which was intended to amuse educated visitors, runs:

This house hates sadness, loves peace,
Offers baths, recommends the pastoral life,
And would like to have honest men as guests.

Under the cartouche, there are bas reliefs which show two sphinxes, back to back, as symbols of intelligence, and also of the pleasures of the flesh. The sphinxes have faces of beautiful, alluring women. The space between them is filled by a large conch, as a symbol of water, and at the same time Venus, since the goddess of beauty was born from the waves. On the conch, between the haunches of the sphinxes, following through the same playful tone, there is the head of a grinning satyr. On the same wall, there are medallions on two side with symbolic attributes of Apollo, the god of poetry and beauty, and Mercury, who advocated reconciliation and was possessed of the gift of oratory. Thus from the very beginning the purpose of the pavilion was conveyed in the fullest possible Baroque style.

On the northern side, another inscription, which is no longer in existence, proclaimed:

Muses, dryads, nymphs, Ceres and Apollo the shepherd,
Pray come to inhabit this house,
May Minerva penetrate it.

This building was not merely a bath house, but also a place for social encounters, and for brief stays. The house was also called the Hippocrene, which according to the mythology of the ancient Greeks, as a fountain on Mt. Helicon, was a symbol of poetic inspiration. The mythological fountain was guarded by the Muses of Apollo, the protector of the arts. In Lubomirski's pavilion, the Hippocrene was a fountain put up in the central, round room richly embellished with stucco in the form of conchs and sculpted representations of dolphins, dragons, or "wild creatures" – probably satyrs, and water nymphs. In the walls of this room, there were four niches from which water spouted over the heads of those present into a basin in the centre. The atmosphere, as we can imagine, was reminiscent of Baroque grottos in Italian gardens, and indeed the room was called the Grotto.

At present the room features a décor dating from the times of Stanislaus

9

Augustus. But there are still three chambers that have preserved their original design.

The first of these is the vestibule with two niches in the main wall. The niches contain statues. One of them is Mars in Repose *(Mars Requiescens)* with Amor at his feet summoning him to battle, perhaps in the lists of love. The second sculpture, originally probably without its sceptre and laurel wreaths, symbolized the "age of happiness". The two statues conveyed the general idea of the function of the Bath House as a haven of tranquillity. Later, the female figure was provided with the inscription *Polonia Florescens"*, which changed the above-mentioned idea and was supposed to mean that now, when Mars, the god of war, rests, Poland experiences prosperity. The walls of the vestibule are tiled, which suggested that one entered a garden pavilion rather than a palace.

The left-hand door leads into the Bacchus Room where a stone portal decorated with flowers and butterflies has been preserved, as well as, presumably, an original, large stone fireplace, which also heated the adjoining room. Above the fireplace you can see a picture showing Silenus, Bacchus' attendant, in the company of Bacchantes, painted in the studio of the Flemish painter Jacob Jordaens the Elder. The walls of the room are tiled and the fashion for such decoration must have come from the Netherlands. The third seventeenth-century chamber is the adjoining bathroom, which was the original Bath House that gave the name to the entire pavilion and then the park. In the southern corners of the chamber there were two sunken baths. The walls still feature original tiles and a unique group of bas-reliefs illustrating Ovid's *Metamorphoses*. The motifs of water present in the decoration were appropriate for this chamber, and the same is true of numerous conchs that can be seen in the ornamentation of the walls and ceiling.

To the east of the Bath House there was a geometrically laid out garden, recreated today, with ornamental flower beds with path arranged like rays of a star. The garden, imitating a French layout popular at that time, was probably designed by Tylman van Gameren.

On 20 August 1690, Ujazdów was visited by an Italian poet, Giovanni Faginoli, who noted in his diary that "there is a splendid bath house there, built in a truly regal taste."

In the next century, the Bath House and associated buildings were to be greatly altered. In 1720, Ujazdów was leased to Augustus II, the King of Poland and Elector of Saxony. The new lessee undertook major landscaping of the area below the escarpment, laying out the royal or Piaseczyński canal. This canal, although a little shorter than the original version, is still in existence today. In the Bath House itself, some of the rooms acquired tiled floors.

Augustus II also laid out the Ujazdów Stations of the Cross. Along the avenue (today's Ujazdowskie Avenue) that led from the square which later became known as Trzech Krzyży (Three Crosses) Square, to the Belvedere, shrines were built as the Stations of the Cross. Near the Belvedere, the route led downhill along the side of the escarpment, and then later climbed uphill through the present area of the Botanical Gardens, where there were three crosses and a chapel with Christ's sepulchre. The whole route was completed in 1724-32 according to a design by Joachim Daniel Jauch. Augustus II funded this project with the intention of winning favour with the inhabitants of Warsaw.

Finally, Augustus II intended to make alterations to the Ujazdów Castle, but almost none of the planned changes were introduced. Not much changed under his successor to the throne, Augustus III, who in the area below the escarpment organized hunting expeditions for animals brought in cages from the Lithuanian forests. These hunts, to which large numbers of guests flocked, were bloody slaughters of defenceless animals.

In the 1730's, the Belvedere was completely converted. The old villa built in the previous century had by now probably disappeared entirely. It may have been destroyed by fire, or perhaps demolished. In its place, a palace was erected. This was a brick building, rectangular in layout. It was one storey high and had two-storey projections with triangular gables, and a tiled mansard roof. Its architecture was modest, but it was within the conventions of the Rococo style which was fashionable in Warsaw under Augustus III. Upstairs, there was a reception room two floors high. The courtyard had outbuildings on both sides. The reconstruction of the Belvedere was ordered by Józef Pac, and the task was entrusted to Józef Fontana, who was in his day a famous Warsaw architect, and the father of Jakub Fontana, Stanislaus Augustus' architect.

In 1748, some of the land lying below the escarpment which belonged to the Belvedere, was ceded to Heinrich Brühl, the renowned minister of the Saxon kings. Brühl surrounded this territory, which was in the shape of an irregular quadrilateral, by a canal. A decorative pavilion was supposed to stand in the middle, but this project was never put into effect. Apparently, this all powerful minister wanted to live as well as work next door to the monarch.

In the same year, 1748, the Belvedere became the property of the Lubomirski family, and then later passed into the hands of Castellan Wincenty Karaś, a friend of Stanisław Poniatowski, the father of the future king.

The accession to the throne of Stanislaus Augustus (Poniatowski) in 1764 marked the beginning of a new era in the history of Ujazdów, Łazienki and the Belvedere. Even before his coronation, Poniatowski, as the Grand Carver of Lithuania, bought Ujazdów together with the area of the old Animal Reserve which was attached to it. He began to reconstruct the Ujazdów Castle, which he intended to turn into a private summer residence. An extra storey was added at the back and front, and at the front this was crowned with an onion dome. The converted interiors acquired new rooms: Chinese studies designed by Jean Pillement; a palm decorated library, designed by Efraim Schroeger; an Apollo room in the eastern projection on the first floor; and underneath this, the "salla Terenna" containing paintings by Bernardo Bellotto called Canaletto. The walls of the main staircase were covered with painted illusionist architecture by Łukasz Smuglewicz. Another interior worth noting was the chapel in the tower, decorated by the columns that held up the dome. We know that the building contained a theatre, and that the painter Carlo Quaglio was employed there, although we do not know what the auditorium looked like. Along with these alterations in the castle, one-storey annexes were built in the front courtyard. Although we know the names of many artists who were employed here, we cannot be entirely sure who was the chief architect, for it may have been either Domenico Merlini or August Moszyński. Or indeed, the person in charge might have been Jakub Fontana, or even the king himself, who certainly at least discussed every detail, and who usually imposed his views on the architect who actually made the drawings.

While these alterations were being made to the Ujazdów Castle, there was also intensive work being carried out in the area of the Animal Reserve below the escarpment and in the foreground of the castle. The Animal Reserve, or in other words, an ordinary overgrown wood, was now being turned into a garden. Straight avenues which intersected at circuses were built across the area. On the level upland in front of the castle, leading straight from it, a five-kilometre approach drive was set out which stretched as far as Wola. Nearer to the residence, a network of straight avenues was laid out which met, like the rays of a star, in round circuses. This urban plan was later called the Stanislaus Axis. The avenues and circuses were laid out amidst arable land and lined with lime trees. They became the skeleton for a new district which was gradually built up and which today forms a major fragment of Warsaw's town centre. Who was the author of this town-planning project? It may have been August Moszyński, the Crown Carver, who was in charge of the reconstruction of the castle, or perhaps Schroeger. But the main author seems to have been Stanislaus Augustus himself. Gradually, by means of purchase and exchange, he extended his Ujazdów estates. He turned his attention also to the Belvedere, which he purchased in 1767. In the northern outbuilding of this palace, the new owner set up a Royal Porcelain Manufactory. Moszyński – a man who had a wide range of talents and knowledge – was the organizer of this enterprise. The finding of suitable clay in nearby Mokotów determined the choice of the Belvedere as the site of production. The manufactory was opened on 30 December 1768. Its first director was Franz Joseph Schütter, a Bavarian by origin, who acquired this position mainly thanks to his beautiful wife, who enjoyed the monarch's special favour. Unfortunately, Schütter did not know enough about the production of porcelain, and besides, the raw material was not of the best, so that the first attempts were not successful. As a result, under pressure from Moszyński, Stanislaus Augustus gave up the production of porcelain and in 1770 began the manufacture of coarser pottery. This was the right decision. Pottery marked "Varsovie", or with the letter "B", popularly known as "belvederes", was exceptionally successful and highly artistic. In line with the currently prevailing fashion for chinoiserie, which clearly affected the king's undertakings in this period in the area of the Łazienki (as we shall see shortly), the products of the Belvedere manufactory were fairly freely modelled in both form and decoration on Eastern porcelain. The Belvedere faience was primarily intended to serve the needs of the court, and included everyday objects, such as bowls and jugs, as well as urinals and bidets which were indispensable in every residential apartment. The Belvedere manufactory also produced white tiles from which stoves in the style of vases or "pyramids" were built. The insides of the fireplaces in the royal study in the Bath House were also lined with coloured Belvedere tiles. In the Łazienki Palace you can find moreover candleholders, writing implements, like inkwells and sand trays, small and large flower vases – white flowers on a sapphire background, or coloured on a white background – and other decorative objects made "from Belvedere faience". Another item made in the manufactory was a great dinner service, the *service turc*, which had 160 pieces. This service, intended for the Sultan Abdul Hamid, was handed to the Turkish envoy, Bey Numan, who returned to Turkey in 1777. Another service of the same kind was made for Stanislaus Augustus. One plate from this service can be admired today in the Bedroom in the Palace on the Lake. Belvedere pottery found purchasers among Varsovians and visitors, who could buy them in the store of the Wasilewski house in Krakowskie Przedmieście Street. The Belvedere Palace itself was not altered, and retained the form it had been given in the 1730's.

Let us now return to the Ujazdów Castle, where work on the alterations took years, and unfortunately, to the king's disappointment, without bringing the hoped-for results. Finally, the king limited the scope of further work, and then put a stop to it altogether. Moszyński, blamed for incompetence in supervision of the building work, lost his post in 1772.

In this period, the king turned his attention to the Bath House pavilion standing in the garden below the escarpment and began to convert it into a summer residence. The building was redecorated, some of the rooms in neo-classical style. These new royal apartments were shown in cross-sections of the building drawn in 1776 by Jan Chrystian Kamsetzer, which were lost during the second world war. The most impressive room was the Bedroom, which later became the Dining Room. It was decorated with red and yellow stucco. Twelve oval portraits of members of the royal family hung on the walls. Over the fireplace, there was a double portrait of the parents of Stanislaus Augustus. Thus, before he fell asleep, the king could look at images of his nearest and dearest.

Another important apartment was the Drawing Room which was in the shape of an elongated octagon (this was later turned into the Solomon Room). The Baroque stucco on the ceiling was not touched, but the walls were lined with stucco and mirrors. Over the side doors there were busts of the king and of Lubomirski, who had built the Bath House, in which way the king paid honour to the previous owner of the building.

It seems that the king wished to continue the main outlines of the original concept for the immediate surroudings of the pavilion on the island. The terrace round the Bath House, a summer villa-style pavilion, was adorned with statues of nymphs and satyrs which were supposed to bring to mind the legend of Arcadia, the land of happiness. Some of these sculptures stand today in front of the Old Orangery. Near the Palace on the Lake you may still see statues of satyrs, while on the terrace itself there are two groups of sculptures. One of them represents "a water nymph snatching a bunch of grapes from the hands of a satyr", and the other shows "Hermaphroditos spurning the nymph Salmakis". These were already in place in 1776, and were produced, like those mentioned above, in the royal workshop.

The king's establishment of the Bath House as a summer residence took place at the time of the first partition of Poland (1772). For a while, in the atmosphere of national defeat, the king ceased to have visions of great royal residences like the Warsaw or Ujazdów castles. He retired to the quiet of the garden and concentrated on projects on a more intimate scale, which allowed him to forget temporarily the cares of government. But it would seem that it was not only for this reason. We must remember that there was currently a fashion for escape from grand residences to small, semi-pastoral villas and gardens. Izabela Lubomirska built herself a villa in Mokotów, Prince Adam Czartoryski and his wife escaped to a villa at Powązki, and the king's brother Kazimierz to a villa at Solec. Unlike these, Stanislaus Augustus did not need to buy new land outside the town, since the garden he already owned was sufficiently wild and abandoned to serve as his country retreat.

Twelve years later, in his description of the gardens of Warsaw and district, Szymon Bogumił Zug, a well-known Warsaw architect in the days of Stanislaus Augustus, recalled that early work carried out in the Łazienki.

The garden was "open to all and very much frequented, even when the king is in residence here in the summer. At the beginning of the present reign, it was a marshy wood, planted with alders, with canals and ponds in a state of total disrepair". The area "then served only as pasture for the beasts that were raised there, and one of the king's huntsmen kept an inn there. The present king, having bought this place from Prince Lubomirski, spared no expense on improving it and on clearing the air which was affected by miasmata from stagnant water. With this in mind, all the rotten old alders were felled, and replaced by all manner of deciduous, coniferous and resinous trees, clumps or avenues of which create a pleasant impression. All kinds of walks were made, as well as new lakes and ponds. Through the felling of trees in the damp avenues, from raised places new views were opened up onto charming objects and the surrounding districts like Wilanów, Mokotów, or Czerniaków".

The Łazienki, which was the name that was ever more often used for the old Animal Reserve, began to be filled with visitors. The king ordered an inn to be built for the Warsaw public at the entrance to the garden from the present Myśliwiecka Street. This is still standing today, although in a state of disrepair. It was at first a single-storey building with a second storey only in the central part. It had a high, tiled roof. There are still metal hoops for tying up horses in the base of the building. Inside, there was a billiard table, and the benches for the guests were fixed to the walls, so that in moments of excitement after drinking tankards of beer, they would not be used as instruments for settling arguments. The inn was popular and had many visitors. It was already in place in 1778, when the Livonian Friedrich Schultz wrote: "On the Solec side a large building stands to the fore, containing a restaurant, always ready for small parties, and taking larger gatherings to order. There is plenty of room for picnics in large number, and the innkeeper willingly supplies dishes, wine and dainties for them. There are private rooms for more serious meetings. In a word, there is everything here which every kind of passer-by can desire, as he drinks in the view of the charming garden. The bowers and shady alcoves around this building are full, especially on Sundays and holidays, of perpetually merry guests of the middling sort".

Since the Bath House had become the monarch's summer residence, which was visited by the court and numerous guests, there was a need to build nearby a corps-de-garde, or in other words, a building to house the king's personal escort. The place chosen was to the west of the king's house, and it was erected in 1774, in an interesting pyramid shape. It was a square, brick building covered on the outside with turf. Its designer was probably Jan Chrystian Kamsetzer, Merlini's younger assistant. The Corps-de-Grande was at the same time both a memorial and a building for use. It was the first building which could be seen from the windows of the Bath House, and must have appeared to viewers to be a mausoleum.

At the same time, the White Cottage was built in the Łazienki. We do not know when work on the construction began, but we do know that in 1774 it was already roofed and in 1775-78 its interiors were being finished. Luckily, this building has mostly preserved its original appearance. It was small and in shape was related to the garden villa type of architecture. It was intended as a short-term summer residence. Therefore, it was simple and straightforward, lacking monumental elements, and possessed a light and intimate charm. It is square, and all the side are identical, decorated with rustication and a parapet. The building is topped by a belvedere on the roof. It dates from the early phase of neo-classicism, but the shape of the windows on the first floor, with a segmental arch coping, reflects late Rococo. The use of timber for the parapet balustrade was dictated by a wish not to overload the building with stone, since it was sited on marshy terrain. This was also the reason why the building rests on extremely thick foundation walls. Compared with the old Bath House, the White Cottage was a modern building. It was, however, similarly situated: on an island, surrounded by canals. Apparently the king liked Tylman's design and decided to create its counterpart in the western area of the garden below the escarpment. The building, which in the times of Stanislaus Augustus stood on the edge of the wooded territory, was perfectly visible from the Ujazdów Castle, which inclines one to think that work on its construction was begun earlier, while the king was still making alterations to the castle. It was a modern villa situated near to the main residence. The well-appointed interiors suggest that the king intended the White Cottage for his personal use, although later, according to legend and the few mentions in writing, Elżbieta Grabowski, Stanislaus Augustus' morganatic wife, lived here, and also the king's sisters, Izabela Branicka, the wife of the castellan of Cracow, and Ludwika Maria Zamoyska, as well as the king's sister-in-law, Teresa Hurula née Kińska, the widow of Andrzej Poniatowski, the Austrian general, and mother of Prince Józef Poniatowski.

The building was designed by Merlini. Inside, around the staircase in the centre, there were richly decorated rooms intended for various purposes. The largest was the dining room, the walls of which were entirely covered with grotesque paintings by Jan Bogumił Plersch in 1777. These paintings symbolize the four elements, the times of day and human labour. Among these simple, everyday themes, there are motifs taken from Freemasonry, which was understandable here, since the king belonged to the movement. In the middle of the main wall, there is a semi-circular niche with a statue of Venus, an original classical statue which the king purchased in Rome. The sconces on the walls are adorned with the heads of rams, which was no coincidence, since the ram was the beast of Venus. This room was undoubtedly Stanislaus Augustus' pride. Perhaps he invited here his regular Łazienki guests, and maybe also those who came to his famous "Thursday Dinners", at which artists, authors and reformers discussed important matters of state. The Dining Room adjoins the Drawing Room, decorated with painted views of China. The smaller paintings are in fact original Chinese wallpaper glued to the walls, while on the main wall there is a painting on plaster by Plersch. In connection with this chinoiserie, of which there was so much in the Łazienki under Stanislaus Augustus, we might point out that according to contemporary beliefs, the Chinese were a people who knew how to live in accord with nature, and the idea of a return to nature was one which had caught the imagination of the whole of Europe, under the tutelage of Jean Jacques Rousseau.

There were also elements of chonoiserie in the decoration of the Bedroom. According to those who compiled the inventory of 1783, the walls were "an imitation of Chinese birds of various species sitting in trees and on the wing, and also painted butterflies". The author of these paintings was Jan Ścisło. Alongside the birds flying or sitting in bushes or trees, there were hunting weapons painted on the panelling and doors. This may have been an allusion to pastoral life in the bosom of nature, or perhaps to the old Animal Reserve, the tradition of which Stanislaus Augustus kept up by fencing off a nearby area and keeping pheasants and ostriches there. But probably these symbols had yet another meaning, especially here in the Bedroom. Emblems of hunting could constitute an invocation to the goddess of the hunt, Diana, who watched over young boys and girls and also married love. The bed, which stands in an alcove, and is the original bed from the times of Stanislaus Augustus, is covered with fine carving. The back has the motif of kissing doves and the attributes of Eros, a quiver with arrows against the background of a conch. This is an expressive allusion to the character of this room, whose occupant did not usually sleep here alone. The same serene atmosphere prevails in the Octagonal Study, where the wall decoration by Plersch and Ścisło suggests the interior of a wooden bower interwoven with branches of climbing roses, which, as the flower of Aphrodite, were the symbol of love. Various views open up from this bower, modelled on the paintings of Claude Joseph Vernet. On the first floor of the White Cottage, the vestibule claims special attention. Its walls have oval medallions with images of small Eros. Their gestures, and the presence of kissing doves, convey an unambiguous message about the character of this place. One other residential chamber deserves mention: its walls are decorated with painted garlands of meadow flowers which surround closely hung prints showing various mythological scenes.

Close the the south side of the White Cottage, a sundial held by a seated satyr was placed in 1777. In the same year, an outbuilding was erected to house the kitchens and servants' quarters.

Before the White Cottage was completed, another pavilion was being built at the other, eastern end of the Łazienki. This was also the work of Merlini, and was known as Myślewice, since once upon a time the village of Myślewice had existed here. We do not know exactly when construction work was begun, but we do know that in 1775 the walls were already standing. It was originally conceived as a square building, and what is now the central, main part of the house was built first, with a great niche at the front with a conch shell at the top and two statues representing Zephyr and Flora by Giacomo Monaldi. The building was two storeys high and was perfectly visible from the windows of the Ujazdów Castle. Myślewice, together with the Bath House and the White Cottage, formed a group of three villas, and the king, who liked to vary the routine of his stays at the Łazienki, would live in several buildings in the course of one season.

Myślewice soon proved too small for the needs of its owner. The villa was extended with side wings, each forming half of a semi-circle. The wings were one storey high with two-storey pavilions at the end. In 1783, a second storey was added to the wings, and thereby the villa became a palace, which has remained almost unchanged to the present day. Its facade is decorated with a great conch shell. The roof has an original shape showing Chinese influence. The decoration as a whole represents the early phase of neo-classicism with Rococo undertones. The building has also preserved the original interiors. Among these, we should note the Dining Room with views of Venice, Rome and the Vatican painted by Plersch, and an original marble fireplace, on which there stands a bust of Madame du Barry, the mistress of Louis XV of France, produced by Augustine Pajou in 1773. The bust has occupied this place since the eighteenth century. The decoration of the bathroom is also original. The walls are stucco and the ceiling is decorated with a painting by Plersch which represents a theme suggested at the entrance to the building. This is a composition with Flora, the goddess of spring and flowers, and Zephyr, her envoy, the mild wind which pollinates the flowers, and introduces a mood of the pastoral and of love.

The wall paintings have been preserved also in certain other rooms of the Myślewice palace. In one of the rooms in the western wing, we may admire a series of fantastic views of ancient ruins painted against the background of a romantic landscape. These were by Antoni Herliczka, Jan Klemens Branicki's painter, borrowed by the king. Herliczka was also almost certainly the author of the paintings in the Small Study on the second floor – of grey-green panels interspersed with medallions containing personifications of art and learning.

And so the most important buildings which the king constructed from scratch in the 1770's were the White Cottage and Myślewice. They are the showpieces providing evidence of the king's good taste, and of the talents of his artists.

But despite the modern facilities and comfort of the new pavilions, the king continued to reside in the old Bath House, and was in no hurry to leave it. Doubtless he was detained here by the incomparable situation of the building on an island surrounded by water. It was possible before and after receptions to indulge, together with the lords and ladies of the court, in his favourite pastime of taking a boat through the ponds and canals. There was a whole fleet of richly ornamented boats with canopies. In 1775, the king ordered a decorative staircase to be built down to the water on the northern tip of the island. The longer he lived in the Bath House, the more determined the king became to adapt the building as the main villa. The number of rooms had to be increased, and the bedroom had to be removed to the first floor, since it was too damp downstairs. The first floor was therefore extended, without, however, changing the picturesque northern facade which would have been difficult to alter. The building became two storeys high on the southern, eastern and western sides, while remaining a single storey on the north. The extensions to the facade were covered with paintings by the indispensable Plersch.

The whole was not at all uniform and somewhat strange. Despite this, it remained unchanged in this form for seven years and was not criticized by contemporaries. The Swiss traveller, Johann Bernolli, wrote in 1778: "The Bath House is a small but beautiful royal summer palace in an extensive park which thanks to its numerous little streams, ponds, bridges, bowers and many other charming features has become a tempting place for walks, where in addition the owner of the nearby café will provide refreshing drinks to quench your thirst at tables and benches in the open air". The English traveller, William Coxe, who visited Warsaw at the same time, noted that "obedient to the gracious invitation of the king, we set off ... for one of the royal villas, lying three miles from Warsaw in the midst of a vast park. The house is small, for on the ground floor there is only a drawing room and four other chambers together with the bathroom, from which the name, La Maison de Bain, is taken. Upstairs, there are the same number of rooms as below, and all arranged quite exquisitely. ... After the reception, we strolled in the park, to see the other villas in which the king resides from time to time. Although they are constructed in various styles, each of them is marked by great taste and elegance. The king loves architecture and himself drew all the plans for the buildings, and even made the drawings for the interior decoration of particular apartments".

The Study was on the first floor on the southern side. Its main wall had a painting by Plersch with a view of Canton. Thus the king when he sat at his desk had on the one hand a picture of a Far Eastern town, and on the other, through the window, a view of his own garden with a canal straight ahead, and through avenues cut in the trees, distant vistas to Mokotów and Czerniaków. The Bedroom was adjacent on the western side, and where it had been before, the king made a Dining Room in which he received enlightened guests at his Thursday Dinners.

Merlini left the northern facade unchanged, but added at the sides two Chinese galleries, covered with green and gilded roofs, as well as bridges – the western one leading to the Royal Promenade which had been laid out in 1778. This promenade was a broad, straight avenue running between two canals and linking the Bath House with the White Cottage. On each side of the avenue there was wooden lattice work overgrown with Indian acacias. The promenade was crossed by a public road to Wilanów, which formed a natural obstacle to careless strollers. This difficulty was overcome by building a bridge on pillars over which strollers from the Bath House could walk to reach the White Cottage, while carriages passed underneath. A large Chinese-style bower on top of the bridge commanded fine views of the surrounding area. This construction, covered with metal sheeting painted green and gold, was designed by Kamsetzer and built in 1778-80. The bridge was the largest example of imitation Chinese architecture in contemporary Warsaw, and formed a link between the Chinese galleries in the Bath House and the similar ones that were built in this period at the White Cottage. It was therefore a picturesque architectural composition which added a new note of interest to the previous arrangement of avenues and waterways in the park. As the reader will remember, a straight waterway ran south from in front of the Łazienki, which had been in existence since the times of Stanisław Herakliusz Lubomirski. In the section nearest to the Bath House, it became a regulated river running from a spring in the area of the later Królikarnia Palace a couple of miles away. Probably as early as the seventeenth century, at the point where the irregular stream entered the straight waterway a step forming a waterfall had been built. Stanislaus Augustus decided to improve the scale of this element in the park, and had a much larger waterfall over boulders built. In order to achieve the desired effect, he ordered the digging of a fairly large lake (today the upper lake), which would form a reservoir to increase the impetus of the water that would fall to the waterway. The project was completed in 1779.

Much more was going on in the Łazienki in the 1770's. In 1777, the Hermitage was scorched by lightning, and shortly thereafter work was begun on rebuilding it as a home for Sophie Henriette Lhullier, the king's mistress. The décor of the interiors of this villa recalled that of the White Cottage. The building was covered with a mansard roof. A garden was laid out around the house, with a dense network of winding avenues, which, according to the contemporary mode, was in the Anglo-Chinese style, and was also known as the Wild Promenade. The Hermitage, which had once stood in the midst of a wood, on marshy land, was now much more exposed in the middle of a garden. It lay almost at the main entrance to the king's island residence, from which it was visible. Near the Hermitage, a small building containing a kitchen was built.

The royal villa, the Bath House on the island, also had a kitchen in a separate building. As a rule, kitchens were housed in separate buildings, in order to protect gentlemen's residences from fire. It was in kitchens that fires broke out most frequently. There was smoke in them and in addition they were usually black with flies. The first kitchen attached to the Bath House stood probably on the site of the later Officer Cadets' School, and dated back to the days of the Saxon kings, or perhaps even to those of Stanisław Herakliusz Lubomirski. It looked like a small manor house. Stanislaus Augustus also made use of this kitchen. In 1778, Merlini added a single-storey annexe at right angles to the northern corner of the building, which was intended as living quarters. For example, Paweł Tremo, the keeper of Stanislaus Augustus' kitchens, lived here, as did Antoni Luciński, the royal cup-bearer. This annexe constitutes today the northern wing of the Officer Cadets' School, although, of course, it originally looked different, and had a mansard roof.

At more or less the same time, in 1779-80, yet another pavilion was erected, known as the Trou-Madame. This was intended for the game of this name, which consisted in throwing ivory dice through marble goalposts. It stood to the west of the Bath House and Corps-de-Garde and was shaped like a pyramid. It was rectangular in outline, with a Chinese-style roof, and its walls were painted with views of forests, which created an astonishing effect since the building stood amidst real trees. The building was almost certainly designed by Merlini and decorated by Plersch.

What, meantime, was happening at the Belvedere? The pottery manufactory was still in existence, despite difficulties with bringing water to the site. In 1776, for this reason, there was even a scheme for the transfer of the manufactory to another location, preferably somewhere closer to the Vistula. The king was also advised against making the Belvedere into a royal residence: "It is unlikely that this palace could be adapted as a gentleman's residence; it would be better to pull it down in order to build another, for which a design can be drawn through the winter". However, there was no immediate start on a general reconstruction. The palace was set aside as quarters for the royal guests. The walls of the rooms were thickly hung with paintings. It is enough to say that more than 700 paintings were to be found here, including a large number of portraits of well-known Polish figures. Since the production of pottery was not profitable, the king leased the manufactory to Schütter, who, however, was unable to make the business pay, and in 1783 it ceased to exist. The only architectural trace of this enterprise was until recently the building known as the Small Mill in which the clay was prepared for firing. This was situated on the other side of the road, in front of the palace.

Along with all his other interests. Stanislaus Augustus was particularly fond of the theatre. He was, let us recall, responsible for the opening of a national theatre in 1765, and later for the construction of a theatre at Krasińskich Square. He also set up the first theatre in a private residence of his in the Ujazdów Castle. Later, the king organized performances in his brother Kazimierz's theatre at Solec, not very far from the Łazienki. But when this theatre passed from the hands of the king's brother in 1782, it was seen as a matter of great urgency to set a similar one in the Łazienki. There was no time to put up a new building. A pre-existent structure had to be converted for this purpose and the choice fell on the Trou-Madame. So Merlini and Plersch adapted this building as a court theatre known as the Commedia or Small Theatre. Its outward appearance was only slightly altered. The auditorium was given seven rows of benches. The stage, which had a curtain, scenery and an effects room, served the king for six seasons. The old Trou-Madame pavilion still exists today within the walls of the New Corps-de-Garde, which today houses a café called Trou-Madame, thus referring to the original purpose of the building.

We have now entered the 1780's, the period of the greatest royal activity in the area of the Łazienki and Ujazdów. In the previous decade, the Łazienki was full of Chinese motifs. Now these themes were abandoned, and there was a tendency to return to those of Ancient Rome. One signal of an approaching fashion for this trend was yet another – and this time radical – rebuilding of the Bath House in 1784. It was now to become a neo-classical villa in which all the sides were to be of the same height, crowned with a belvedere which covered the original skylight in the cupola. As it happened, only the southern facade acquired a new appearance. Two segments were added to the old Bath House. They were linked by a four column portico *in antis* and the whole was given a common entablature and a balustraded parapet with stone statues symbolizing the Four Seasons. The design was by Merlini and the statues were sculpted by Andreas le Brun. Although it only partly implemented the king's ideas, this facade of hewn stone retains to the present day its simplicity and style, creating a uniform impression of balance and harmony. It is light and picturesque, in the spirit of the then prevailing neo-classical style.

In the course of the alterations, the Dining Room was extended to the south side, and the new part was divided from the old by pairs of stucco columns. Its colour scheme was changed to white and red. The fireplace, which was previously on the end wall, was now moved to the eastern wall in the new part. During this operation, the plate was broken, which must have provoked the king's anger. The cracked plate was riveted together and has remained in that state to the present day. There was general admiration for the new facade of the Bath House. The work was carried out quickly. As early as 4 September 1784, the court painter, Marcello Bacciarelli, who was overseeing the whole scheme, wrote to the king: "I have the honour to convey to Your Highness the news that the facade of the Łazienki has been completed." The construction of the new facade was to be the beginning of further alterations to the Bath House, but at this point the work was broken off for several years. The king put all his efforts into re-designing the gardens on a south-north axis. The straight canal that had run south to the waterfall was now turned into a large southern lake (the lower lake) with a picturesque shoreline. Shortly thereafter, the old pond on the northern side was changed into a broad and equally irregular lake which stretched as far as Agrykola Street. And therefore the layout of the gardens was completely changed, reflecting the fashion for the English, landscaped garden. The Bath House was at the centre of the new scheme, and was now perfectly visible from south and north above the surface of the water. Finally, the Bath House had assumed the role of the main royal villa.

This clearly stressed compositional axis was, in line with the ruling fashion for the irregular, broken by an island with old trees. In 1785, a stage was set up on this island with permanent scenery in the form of a rocky grotto, and it was called the Theatre on the Island. On the land side, a summer amphitheatre was constructed. This auditorium, which had three rows of benches, was covered in 1788 with a canvas roof on poles, which protected the audience from the vagaries of the climate. In any event, the king was able to entertain here a much larger number of guests than in the Small Theatre. The most original element in the new theatre was the separation of the audience from the stage by water, which could be made use of in what took place on the stage. After the performance, the king would invite his guests to dance in the Turkish House, known also as the Public Salon.

This wooden building was situated near the amphitheatre, and on the outside was in oriental style, while inside it was attractively decorated in neo-classical style. It was designed by Kamsetzer and built in 1786.

Eighteenth century gardens, and so also the Łazienki, were decorated with orange trees placed outside in the summer. In the winter, they were kept in special buildings known as orangeries. It was therefore necessary for the Łazienki to have one of these. Designed by Merlini, it was built in 1785-88, in the western part of the garden, where the escarpment ran a little further to the west. The main southern facade, divided by pilasters and arcaded doors, is neo-classical in its simplicity. Inside, it contains a long room intended for plants. Because of the function and scale of this building, it was known in the days of Stanislaus Augustus as the Great Orangery. This basic part of the building was abutted on the northern side by two wings, of which the west wing contained servants quarters and guest rooms, while the east wing was to contain a theatre. The theatre wing has been preserved to the present day in an almost unaltered state, and is one of the few buildings of this kind that have survived in the world. The square auditorium was intended for two hundred, and at the level of the first floor is surrounded by nine boxes divided by pairs of pilasters, between which stand female figures painted by Le Brun, Monaldi and Staggi. The ceiling was decorated with a great painting showing Apollo, the god of the arts, as a reference to the artistic achievements of the reign of Stanislaus Augustus. In order that there should be no doubt that the Łazienki was a shrine to the Muses of Apollo, the king ordered Plersch to paint on the curtain Mount Parnassus, which apparently lay in the Łazienki gardens, since alongside it was the Bath House with the new facade dating from 1784. Unfortunately, this curtain was destroyed in the nineteenth century. In the corners of the ceiling, four medallions were painted with likenesses of, in Stanislaus Augustus' view, the four greatest dramatists, Sophocles, Shakespeare, Molière and Racine. The most interesting element in the painted decoration of the auditorium is the row of illusionist boxes, filled with well-dressed courtiers. This is a fragment of authentic life two hundred years ago, perfectly captured by the artist. Plersch was the author of all the paintings, and also of the king's coat-of-arms above the stage, placed in the centre of the emblem of the Commonwealth of Poland, and held up by two genii of fame – a crest that aroused the admiration of all visitors, for it was executed with such precision that from the auditorium it looked as if carved in stucco. The whole interior was constructed from wood, which ensured excellent acoustics. The walls were covered with polychrome which gave the appearance of marble. The deep stage had, as befitted an eighteenth-century theatre, a raked floor. Some parts of the equipment of the original effects room have also been preserved, for example, wooden troughs for "making thunders", into which stones were thrown from above to produce the required effect. On each side of the stage there were dressing rooms for the actors, linked by a wooden staircase. The theatre's décor was universally admired. One of the invited guests, a Frenchman, the Abbé Renaud who was staying in Warsaw, expressed this as follows: "This happy marriage of the Roman and French styles, just as existed in the fine years of Louis XIV, gives the theatre a striking appearance of greatness and richness." Today, we can say of this interior that it is the showpiece of the Stanislaus style, a concept that art historians use to describe the artistic achievements of his own vision of neo-classicism. The theatre in the Great Orangery, which is now called the Old Orangery, was called the Grand

Theatre to distinguish it from the Small Theatre. It was opened on 8 September 1788 and from that moment on there was intense activity. In front of the building, a garden with sculptures was laid out on the southern side, separated from the park by a low wall. The king intended this to be a kind of open-air museum.

The opening of the theatre was preceded a few days earlier by the unveiling of a statue to John III (Sobieski), which stood beside the three-span bridge which was an extension of the old single-span bridge in Agrykola Street. The bridge was designed by Merlini, and the statue was the work of Franciszek Pinck, who modelled it on the Baroque statue of John III at Wilanów. A rider in armour and a plumed helmet tramples under his horse's hooves two sprawled figures of Turks. With this monument Stanislaus Augustus wanted to arouse anti-Turkish feelings in Poland and draw the country into a military alliance with Russia, hoping that this would enable him to set up a strong Polish army. This intention came to nothing, but the monument remains, and alongside the Bath House Palace is one of the most striking features of Stanislaus Augustus' property.

The new bridge with its statue required a new plan for the shores of the northern lake, which were now straightened to a design by Jakub Kubicki. In this way, the Bath House and the bridge were spatially linked by the surface of the water, and the whole effect must be reckoned one of the most successful of all times. On the day of the unveiling of the statue, Stanislaus Augustus organized a great fête at the Łazienki. An "amphitheatre" for six thousand guests was built near the Great Orangery. Here, knightly contests and tournaments were held. This occasional timber structure was designed by Kubicki, and the gateway was adorned with the coats-of-arms of John III (Sobieski), Poniatowski and of the Commonwealth of Poland. Thirty thousand of the inhabitants of Warsaw came to the celebrations, and sat on the slopes of the escarpment and nearby trees to watch the show.

The crowning of all the king's undertakings in the Łazienki was the transformation of the main Bath House pavilion into a palace. This task was begun in 1788. The Łazienki ceased to be a quiet, pastoral retreat, and became a centre with many functions for the court and a wider public. In the main building, the king, who loved dancing, had to have a large Ballroom, which in fact became the key element in the whole new concept. The Ballroom was designed by Merlini and Kamsetzer. It was the latter who probably had the decisive influence on the form of the northern elevation which in fact became a facade, since the entrance to the palace was along the side of the northern lake. With plans for a spacious Ballroom the island had to be extended to the north, and a monumental split-level terrace was constructed here. The lowest step of the terrace became a berth for boats. The simple northern side of the building was adorned with a colonnaded portico, and its tympanum carried statues symbolizing Peace and Justice. At the sides of the tympanum, there were statues of Pallas Athena, the goddess of Wisdom, and of Achilles, symbolizing Virtue. The whole was decorated with stone pilasters and crowned with a parapet, at the corners of which there were statues representing the four continents. The building was topped with a quadrangular belvedere with sculpted personifications of the four elements: Water, Fire, Air and Earth. All of the new sculptures were from Le Brun's studio. Leonardo Galli sculpted the stone lions which adorned the terrace by the water, while Pinck made the statues of gladiators in combat, which were copies of classical statues. The old Bath House, transformed into a palace, took on an original shape, and at the same time the whole attained an ideal harmony in its proportions. The southern elevation, lit by the sun, became exceptionally picturesque, while the northern front, which remained in the shade, attained a monumental quality. In this exceptional final alteration to the building we can trace the personal influence of the king. At the same time, the interiors became extremely impressive, artistically sublimated and full of symbolism. The largest chamber was the Ballroom, which was white and lighted by two rows of windows. The main elements of the interior, around which the rest was conceived, were two great marble fireplaces in the form of porticos with statues of Apollo and Hercules – copies of classical sculptures which the king had brought from Rome. Beneath Apollo, the symbol of the arts, bend two caryatids, showing folly in the form of King Midas (modelled by Monaldi) and Pride in the form of the satyr Marsias (modelled by Le Brun). Under Hercules, the symbol of Virtue, there are a Centaur (modelled in Rome by Francisco Lazzarini) and Cerberus (modelled by Pinck). The first symbolizes the irresistible force of Nature and the Second, the powers of hell. The overall message of this group of sculptures is therefore plain: Beauty and Virtue triumph in the Ballroom. There is more about the heroes of the room in the bas-reliefs in the upper part of the eastern wall, which show Hercules with his wife Dejanejra and Apollo with Daphne, sculpted by Le Brun. Both of these gods suffered defeat because of a woman. And therefore the presence of this theme here is somewhat difficult to understand. Did the king want to show the fatalistic role of woman, who prevents the triumph of beauty and virtue, or perhaps the apotheosis of the power of woman, who can defeat even the gods? Or perhaps the themes depicted here were meant only as a pretext for showing the figure of the philosopher – king, an advocate of stoicism, who believed that triumph was inextricably linked with defeat, happiness with unhappiness, and that therefore you should always keep your distance to everything in life, retain poise and moderation. The walls of the room are covered with grotesque paintings by Plersch, who here was imitating Raphael's frescoes in the Vatican loggias. They symbolize the elements and also illustrate the concept of time, which in this interior, designed for merriment, is a digression that leads to a moment of philosophical speculation. It is as though the host wished to remind his guests dancing at the palace that this moment of pleasure would – like everything else in life – pass away. The whole sculpted and painted decoration is to show that the only things that make sense in life are art and righteousness. The permeation of the interior with this message gave it a serious character, which is at odds with the function for which it was designed. It is rather a temple with altars to Virtue and Art than a room for dancing, although in the stoics' interpretation, both of these two opposed functions could become one. The Ballroom, with no gilding or colourful elements, is marked by the architectural qualities of the style of Kamsetzer who designed it.

This room was complemented by the Company Room, which played the part of a drawing room and which had colour and gilding. It was also called the Solomon Room, from the hero of the paintings on the walls and ceiling by Bacciarelli. The theme of the biblical king was a popular one in contemporary intellectual circles under the influence of Masonic ideals. Solomon was a model as a builder and as an advocate of peace. The building of the Temple in Jerusalem was the greatest achievement of the young Solomon, while his making of sacrifices to pagan gods as an old man on the instigation of his wife brought about his downfall. These two conflicting sides of the life of the king were reflected in the great paintings covering the main walls of the room. We can trace here a continuation of the theme that was expressed through other motifs in the Ballroom, and also in the figure of Solomon as a wise builder, a reference to Stanislaus Augustus. Maybe the fall of Solomon is also an allusion to the fate of the Polish king. Perhaps it is an accusation levelled at a woman or at himself, perhaps evidence of the triumph of Falsehood over Wisdom, of the victory of illusory beauty over truth and prudence. Perhaps, however, it is a wilful demonstration of adoration of a woman, or self-justification in that even the wise Solomon bowed down, on the instigation of a woman, to false gods. Merlini was the designer of this room; Kamsetzer probably drew out the stucco ornaments for him, and Plersch painted the arabesques. This suite of northern reception rooms ends with a picture gallery with walls lined in green, and this time the author was undoubtedly Kamsetzer alone.

When he had filled the Łazienki with buildings, the king finally abandoned his intention of using the Ujazdów Castle for his own purposes. In 1784, he handed it over to the army. The architect Stanisław Zawadzki converted it into barracks, entirely changing it from its previous style. He removed the domes from the towers, and added two-storey porticos with four columns to the main fronts of the building. He extended the outbuildings and made the whole structure extremely simple in the style of late neo-classicism. This massive building which towered over the Łazienki was shortly to be matched by the king's main residence, the Palace on the Island, which was given a northern facade of equally monumental severity.

This new taste for forms that were less picturesque, stressing instead the effect of noble simplicity, was indicated by the new kitchen building, known as the Grand Annexe. In 1788, the New Annexe, which had been erected eight years earlier, was raised in height. A new kitchen was built on the site of the old in the form of a large two-storey room with many fireplaces, which could serve the large court. To the south, a new wing was added, which was the counterpart to the northern wing, creating a building in the form of a rectangular horseshoe. The main body of the building was crowned with a protruding clock facing west. The whole, now in uniform style, was modest in appearance. The buiding was erected at the same time as the northern facade of the palace. Both were visible from the driveway, and of course the kitchen could not be allowed to compete with the palace itself. The Grand Annexe was probably designed by Kamsetzer. The wings contained servants' quarters and guest rooms, the chambers in the southern wing having a richer décor. It was here that Mme Grabowska had her apartment.

Apart from courtiers and his invited guests, Stanislaus Augustus wanted the people of Warsaw to come to the Łazienki. He did not fence off the park, and it was open to all. It was with the Warsaw public in mind that he ordered a new amphitheatre to be built in place of the old one, this time in brick and stone. This was done in 1790, and the structure was designed by Kamsetzer. The original model for this amphitheatre was the classical theatre at Herculaneum, while the stage decoration was copied from the Roman Forum. An original feature of this design was the fact that the stage was divided from the auditorium by water, and the inclusion in the stage decoration of naturally growing trees, as well as statues as decoration for the auditorium. Originally, there were sixteen seated figures on the parapet of the upper auditorium, which represented the most eminent dramatists in the world, including two Poles, Naruszewicz and Trembecki.

These sculptures were made by Tommaso Righi to a design by Le Brun. They were sculpted in a non-durable material and fairly soon began to decay. Erroneous methods of conservation, using cement, brought these sculptures to such a pitch of ruin that in the inter-war period they were removed and replaced by eight figures sculpted by Stanisław Jakubowski. The remaining original sculptures in the amphitheatre are the Dying Gladiator and Cleopatra, which stand by the side entrances to the auditorium. These were by Pinck who used classical sculptures as his models. The Łazienki amphitheatre is a typical summer theatre intended for a large audience of up to a thousand. Its ceremonial opening took place on 7 September 1791, when the crowds that gathered for the festivities saw the historical ballet, *Cleopatra*, the story of which, involving a naval battle, made it possible to exploit the situation of the theatre on the water and bring "ships" into action. The event has been immortalized in drawings by Jean Pierre Norblin.

At a more or less the same time, a hot-house, known by its German name as the Trebhauz, was built in the Łazienki by the same architect. It was situated in the upper part of the Łazienki, at right angles to Ujazdowskie Avenue, where until recently the village of Ujazdów had stood. Wishing to include these territories in a garden composition, Stanislaus Augustus moved the village to another site, alongside the road leading to Wola. It was this new village that gave its name to the present Nowowiejska (New Village) Street. The Trebhauz is still standing today, although not in its entirety, at the back of the Astronomical Observatory. The original appearance of the building can be recreated from Kamsetzer's architectural plans and from inventories. Thus we know that the middle of the long building was broken up by projections, and the two ends of it were completed by pavilions. On the southern side between these pavilions there were recesses or protruding elements, which contained the glass-houses, and to the north containing the stables and coach houses. It is the central part, which was known as the Royal Room, that has survived. The front is formed by a great window, divided into three parts by Ionic columns. Its central part is wider and turns into a semi-circular arcade. This type of composition is usually known as a Palladian window, popularized by the Italian architect Andrea Palladio in the sixteenth century. Inside, there was a room decorated with grotesque paintings by Plersch. Adjoining the pavilion on both sides, there were hot-houses where figs and pineapples were grown. The gardener's house on the Ujazdowskie Avenue side has also survived. The two sides of the building created different impressions. At the northern front, the main role was played by the simplicity of the walls. To the south, on the other hand, the main stress was placed on using a new material: great sheets of glass. These were necessary in view of the function of the building, but their bold exposure was an unexpected feature, since this kind of service building was usually hidden away in the further reaches of a garden. Stanislaus Augustus accorded this structure considerably greater importance, and included it as part of the composition of the new garden on the terrace of the escarpment.

Shortly afterwards, Kamsetzer was ordered to design a Corps-de -Garde on the eastern shore of the northern lake, beside the main driveway to the palace. This small building, decorated with a stone colonnade and parapet, is designed to match in its monumental appearance the northern front of the palace itself. It was built in 1792.

The monarch constantly had visions of further buildings in the Łazienki.

Many projects got no further than the paper they were written on. He intended to build a Poniatowski family mausoleum in the Łazienki, which would contain his own remains and those of his parents. He also wanted to build a small palace for his sister, Izabela Branicka, but his most important scheme, to which he constantly returned over many years, was that of building the Ujazdów church, and later a Temple of Providence, on the hill beside the Agrykola ravine. Several architects prepared designs over a period of several years, and finally the idea of a round church put forward by Jakub Kubicki and inspired by the Roman Pantheon, won the day. The foundation stone of the Temple of Providence was laid on the anniversary of the passing of the Constitution of 3 May, but political events interfered with these plans.

As well as major buildings, a number of smaller projects were undertaken in the Łazienki, like the Water Tower, known as the Round Tower, erected in 1777, or the pump beside the Agrykola ravine, built in 1784 to a design by Kamsetzer, or the house known as the Mud Hut, situated nearby.

The Łazienki was also filled with sculpture. In 1784, the king ordered four more statues of satyrs to be made, which were placed by the south side of the palace. The corners of the terrace were adorned with statues representing the Vistula and Bug rivers, sculpted by Righi. In the round circus near the Amphitheatre, a marble group was placed showing Tancred and Clorinda, the heroes of Torquato Tasso's *Gerusalemme liberata;* these were by the Pizanis of Florence, and today stand in the gardens at Puławy, awaiting to be brought back to the Łazienki. And finally, there was a group of sculptures standing in the geometrically planned garden in front of the Old Orangery.

Four years after the rebuilding of the palace in 1788, work was begun on extending it again. There was no longer room on the island, and therefore the new elements, in the form of pavilions, stood on the main land, on both sides of the building, and were joined to it by little bridges with colonnaded galleries. The eastern pavilion was the larger of the two, and contained two gateways through which carriages could drive. Guests would arrive by the gateway next to the bridge, and would there alight from their conveyances and enter the palace by the colonnaded gallery, while the carriages made a round of the building and left by the other gateway. The western, smaller pavilion had only one gateway and great, arcaded windows. Inside, there was a high room hung with pictures, known as the Grand Study. The architect of these extensions was Kamsetzer.

Stanislaus Augustus' last undertaking in the Łazienki was a change in the décor of the rotunda of the palace. This work entirely altered the character of the hitherto baroque interior, giving it dignity and solemnity through severe architectural decoration with yellow, grey and white stucco. Statues of the four greatest kings of Poland – Casimir the Great (by Monaldi), Sigismund I, Stephen Báthory (both by Le Brun) and John III (by Pinck) – were placed in niches; over the doors there were three busts of "good" Roman emperors, Titus, Trajan (both by Le Brun) and Marcus Aurelius, which are eighteenth century copies of classical models. On each side of the busts, there are putti modelled by Righi. A Latin inscription from the tenth book of Lucan's *Pharsalia* – *"Utile mundo editi in exemplum"* – explains that all these personages are there "for the benefit of the world and as models". The paintings in the cupola, which represent the four times of the day, are by Plersch. Until recently we did not know about their existence, since in the times of Stanislaus Augustus, they were covered with tondos by Bacciarelli which fitted in better with the new design of the room. Bacciarelli's paintings symbolize the four Virtues: Mars for bravery, Minerva for wisdom, Themis for justice, and Clementia for mercy. The artist did not miss the opportunity to paint a portrait of Stanislaus Augustus himself as Mars, the god of war. Bacciarelli's paintings also survived, but a few years ago, they had to be removed in order to reveal Plersch's paintings, which were deteriorating as a result of the modern heating system in the palace. Currently, Bacciarelli's paintings are to be seen in the conservation exhibition on the first floor of the palace. The Rotunda was Stanislaus Augustus' last achievement, dedicated to his predecessors on the throne who had served Poland best. This room, in the centre of the royal villa, became in a way a pantheon of national glory. But the king was not to see the completed version of the Rotunda. From exile, he sent detailed questions about the progress of the work and directed the affairs of the Łazienki from a distance.

During the lifetime of Stanislaus Augustus, the Łazienki reached a level which bore witness to the high artistic potential of his age. It was open to men of learning and the arts who flocked to this great patron, and it became a centre where modern ideas were formed. During the Four Year Seym which passed the Constitution of 3 May in 1792, the king made the theatre in the Old Orangery available to the troupe run by Wojciech Bogusławski, the founder of the national theatre, who later wrote of this the following: "Our gracious sovereign, in order to save me from losses, ordered that twice a week, Polish plays should be offered in the court theatre in the Łazienki, which were free of charge to the public, and paying for this from his own resources, he provided us with the means of keeping ourselves for many year."

Although the Łazienki was at that time on the outskirts of the city, it played a direct role in the events of the Kościuszko insurrection of 1794. It was from the Ujazdów Castle that the famous Działyński regiment set out, and its armed intervention was decisive in bringing victory in the street fighting in Warsaw. As he left Warsaw, Stanislaus Augustus leased to his butler Franciszek Ryx the land of the Łazienki, but he excluded the palace from the lease. After the death of the king, the Łazienki was inherited by Prince Józef Poniatowski, who, however, invested nothing here. In 1801-04, the Comte de Lille, Louis Bourbon, the brother of the guillotined Louis XVI, who was later to become Louis XVIII, lived here in the summer months. In 1808, to pay his debts, Prince Józef Poniatowski handed the Łazienki over to Onufry Kicki, the king's chamberlain and once close friend. After the death of Prince Józef, the Łazienki was inherited by his sister, Maria Teresa Tyszkiewicz. The Belvedere, on Kicki's death in 1816, became the property of his daughter, Teresa.

In 1817, Mme Tyszkiewicz sold the Łazienki to Tsar Alexander I. From that moment on, for a hundred years, it was the private property of the tsars of Russia, who also called themselves kings of Poland. The Commission for Imperial Palaces looked after the park and buildings, and took real care that everything should be kept in good order. The rarity of the visits of the new owner to Warsaw had a beneficial effect on the Łazienki, for no new building projects were undertaken, and it has – unlike similar complexes in other parts of Europe – retained so much of its original appearance and charm. There were more evident changes in the period of the Kingdom of Poland. For example, in first place, there was a major rebuilding of the Belvedere for the requirements of the Grand Duke Constantine, the brother of the tsar. Work, to a design by Kubicki, lasted from 1815 to 1822. The Rococo palace was turned into a neo-classical building with colonnaded porticos at the front and on the garden side. Single-storey wings were added at right angles to the main structure, and the rooms here were integrated into the main arrangement of the original palace. When one looks at this new Belvedere, one has the impression that the architect was continuing and developing the style which had been created earlier by those working with Stanislaus Augustus. This is not surprising, since Kubicki was once the architect of the king of Poland. The most impressive interiors are the Blue Room, known today as the Pompeii Room, and the Drawing Room, which have both been preserved unchanged to the present day. When the Grand Duke and his Polish wife, Joanna Grudzińska, moved into the Belvedere, it was necessary to provide suitable auxiliary quarters, like stables, carriage houses, and also, as was the custom for major residences, a riding school. These buildings, designed by Kubicki, were situated on the land lying in front of the palace, a little to one side. The stables and carriage houses were completed in 1822. They were shaped like a broken horseshoe, and in the corners, there were higher residential pavilions. Both the pavilions and the wings have been preserved, but the central part was later replaced by a new two-storey building. Alongside these buildings, a riding school was built in 1823-24, with characteristic pointed arched windows, which also survives to the present day. This gives us an interesting example of a marriage of styles: neo-classicism with mock gothic. In the context of work carried out in this period, we should also mention the two-storey high square building of the guardhouse, situated below the escarpment at Belwederska Street. At the back of the palace and to the south, a romantic garden was laid out. The palace terrace was walled around in brick with an iron balustrade. The old church which stood somewhere near the riding school was pulled down. In front of the palace, there was a little island in the lake, and on this a bust of Maria Teodorovna, the mother of the Grand Duke, was placed. There is no trace today of these elements, but we may still admire the Temple of Sibyl and the Egyptian Temple, both probably designed by Kubicki, although we know that Alexandre d'Alfonce also had a hand in the design of the garden. The third of the garden pavilions, the Gothic Orangery, was demolished in 1890. All that remains of it is a bit of the foundations near the White Cottage. All three pavilions, which represented different historical styles, were built at the same time, in 1822. Kubicki's activities in the Łazienki were not confined to the environs of the Belvedere. He was also responsible for the alterations to the Grand Annexe to turn it into the Infantry Cadet School in 1822, for building a stables and carriage house at the manor farm in 1824, and also for altering the old Trou-Madame into the late neo-classical Corps-de-Garde in 1830.

In 1828, a two-storey building was erected in the southern part of the Łazienki manor farm, which was marked by extreme simplicity of style. This was the Invalids' Barracks, probably designed by Wilhelm Heinrich Minter, who designed and supervised the construction of the nearby Hussars' Barracks. The territory of the Łazienki was reduced by the fencing off of the Belvedere Garden, and also in 1848 by the opening of the Botanical Gardens, which covered the terrace of the escarpment between the Agrykola ravine and the old Trebhauz. The hill with the ruins of the foundations of the unbuilt Temple of Providence was also included. In 1820 to

1824, the Astronomical Observatory was built on the southern edge of the Botanical Gardens. The building was designed by Michał Kado, Chrystian Piotr Aigner, and Hilary Szpilowski. It has a columned portico with two superstructures and was built on to the central room of the old Trebhauz. It is a successful linking of two buildings from different epochs. At the same time, the eastern residential pavilion was also built.

In 1828, a boulder was placed on the hill above the Old Orangery and on its uneven surface, Professor Wojciech Jastrzębowski etched a sundial with the aid of an instrument which he had himself invented. It is still there today. Earlier, in 1823, Aigner decorated the old Water Tower with a frieze of ox skulls and a two-column portico at the entrance. In this way, he made the building similar to the tomb of Cecilia Metella near Rome. At this time, two significant buildings from the times of Stanislaus Augustus disappeared from the Łazienki. These were the Chinese Bridge over the Promenade and the pyramid-shaped Corps-de-Garde. The Łazienki, still open to the public, continued to throb with life. The theatre in the Old Orangery and the Outdoor Theatre both experienced a revival. Meanwhile, the ominous Grand Duke Constantine resided in the Belvedere, gathering spies about him and locking up patriots in the cellars.

The Łazienki and the Belvedere were witnesses to the events of November 1830. The students of the Infantry Cadet School in the Łazienki attacked the Belvedere, intending to assassinate the oppressor. This action sparked off a national insurrection, known as the November Uprising. The insurrectionary authorities ordered the Belvedere to be sealed, and Joanna Grudzińska, who inherited it, left it in her will to "the king ... of Poland, whoever he may be". In this way, the Belvedere, like the Łazienki, came into the hands of the tsars of Russia, who also considered themselves to be kings of Poland – Nicholas I, Alexander II, and Nicholas II. When they occasionally visited Warsaw, the tsars preferred to live in the Łazienki or the Belvedere rather than the Royal Castle. Nonetheless, they made no fundamental changes here. It was not until 1846 that an Orthodox church was built on to the western pavilion of the Palace on the Island, covered with a flat cupola designed by Andrzej Gołoński. This architect may also have built the Summer House near the Invalids' Barracks on the manor farm. In 1860, after the Gothic Orangery in the Belvedere Garden, which threatened collapse, had been pulled down, work was begun on a New Orangery in the southern part of the garden. It was designed by Józef Orłowski and Adam Adolf Loeve. This building, which survives to the present day, is glassed on the southern side and at the top has a raised arched segment with half-rosette windows, decorated with sculptures linked thematically with the purpose of the building. These were by Leon Molatyńsk. In the 1860's, the Turkish House, which was in a state of disrepair, was also pulled down, and in 1871 yet another orangery building was erected to the south of the New Orangery. This was intended to house a collection of orange trees purchased from the Radziwiłłs of Nieborów. During the first world war, because the building was inadequately heated, the orange trees died, and after the war this orangery was demolished.

The Łazienki, which often played host to distinguished guests, was also continually visited by the inhabitants of Warsaw. But while it belonged to the Russian tsars, many of the treasures collected by Stanislaus Augustus were removed. When the Russians left Warsaw in 1915, they took with them all the works of art.

When independence was regained, the Łazienki became the property of the state. Under the Treaty of Riga of 1921, most of the works of art taken out of the country by the Russians were returned to their former place. Shortly, work was begun on restoring the Palace on the Island and removing the alterations made under the tsars. The palace was opened to the public, and only occasionally served as a residence for foreign guests of the president. For a time, the famous novelist, Stefan Żeromski, lived in the White Cottage, and General Wieniawa Długoszowski resided in the Myślewice palace. In 1922, Righi's crumbling sculptures were removed from the Amphitheatre, and partly replaced by new ones by Stanisław Jakubowski. From the standpoint of conservation today, this was an unforgivable error. The next mistake was the demolition of the outbuilding of the White Cottage. In 1926, a memorial to Frédéric Chopin, sculpted by Wacław Szymanowski, was placed on the upper terrace of the Łazienki on Ujazdowskie Avenue.

In 1936, the fence separating the Belvedere Garden from the Łazienki was removed. From 1918 the Belvedere was the residence of the Chief of State, Marshal Józef Piłsudski, and after he stepped down in 1922, it became the residence of the President of the Republic.

From 12 to 14 May 1926, the Belvedere and Łazienki were the scene of fighting between Piłsudski's insurgent forces and those loyal to the government. After Piłsudski's death in 1935, a museum dedicated to him was opened in the Belvedere. The Magdeburg House in which Piłsudski had been imprisoned by the Germans during the first world war, was placed near the palace. Earlier, the buildings of the old stables and carriage house had been altered; the main central part was demolished and replaced by a two-storey building.

And then came September 1939. Anti-aircraft guns were set up in the Łazienki, and the collections from the main palace were taken to shelters in the National Museum. After the Germans took the city, the gardens were closed to the public. Together with the Belvedere, the Łazienki became the residence of the Governor General, Hans Frank. In 1940, German soldiers tore down the Chopin memorial and sent it off for scrap, and in 1944, after the crushing of the Warsaw Uprising, they burnt the Palace on the Lake, having first poured petrol all over the interior. They then drilled thousands of holes for dynamite charges in the burnt-out walls, intending to blow the building up. Only chance prevented the complete destruction of the palace. After the war, the walls were made safe, and then work began on rebuilding, which took seventeen years. The architect of this project was Jan Dąbrowski, the work was supervised by Kazimierz Petera, and the interior design was by Marek Kwiatkowski. The palace became a museum of interiors dating from the Enlightenment period. Later, other buildings were reconstructed: the Old Orangery, the White Cottage and the Myślewice Palace. Finally, the whole of the Łazienki was brought together again under one administration, without the Belvedere, which remains the official residence of the head of state.

Today, the Royal Łazienki is a nature reserve, a public park, the scene of museum exhibitions, special exhibitions and numerous concerts and theatre performances. It contains the Belvedere restaurant in the New Orangery, and the Trou-Madame and Amfiteatr cafés. Ufortunately, the northern part of the Łazienki, around the Piaseczyński canal, is not a part of the park. The present appearance of its area clashes with the character of the place. There is however hope that this situation will change, and in the nearest future the two parts of the Łazienki will be reunited.

Let us hope, for the sake of Polish culture, that this will be the case.

Marek Kwiatkowski

This house
hates sadness,
loves peace,
offers baths,
recommends
the pastoral life,
and
would like
to have
honest men
as guests.

King Stanislaus Augustus' monogram on the ceiling of the palace porch

Southern view of the palace

Southern view of the palace

The palace in winter

The Bacchus Room in the Palace on the Island

The porch

A sculpture in the Bacchus Room

The Bacchus Room: A mid-eighteenth century French Baroque clock with a small figure of Bacchus seated on a barrel

The palace: Portrait of Stanisław Heraklisz Lubomirski, the Grand Marshal of the Crown;
late eighteenth century, painter unknown

The bathroom

A sculpture in the bathroom

Bas-relief over the door of the bathroom

The Ballroom

MDCCXCIII

Detail of the wall paintings in the Ballroom

Sculptures on the fireplace in the Ballroom

The palace: Portrait gallery

Detail of the table in the portrait gallery

The Solomon Room

Putto in the Solomon Room

The Solomon Room

The over-door in the Rotunda

The Rotunda in the palace

The king's Dining Room in the palace

Statue of Hebe in the king's Dining Room

Sculpture in the antechamb

Fireplace in the picture
gallery

The picture gallery in the
palace

The royal chapel

The staircase: *Reception of Polish Guests in London*, painted by P.F. Bourgeois, 1791

Antechamber on the first floor

The palace: Portrait of Catherine II in the first floor antechamber

Chronos in the small gallery

View of the small gallery on the first floor

The palace: The balcony room on the first floor

The palace: Study on the first floor

View of the study with a clock

The study: Bronze candlesticks with figures of children on marble bases; France, second half of the eighteenth century

Bedroom on the first floor

First-floor bedroom: Miniature of Stanislaus Augustus, a copy of Bacciarelli's famous portrait (on the reverse, a genuine lock of the king's hair)

The palace: Dressing Room on the first floor

Stanislaus Augustus' curved sword: detail of the hilt and sheath

Pallas Athena

View of the palace from the north

The terrace in front of the Palace on the Island

View of the palace terrace

Sculpture representing the River Bug, by Ludwik Kaufmann, mid-nineteenth century

Detail of the gable on the south side of
the palace

View of the palace from the direction of the Amphitheatre

Marble vase decorated with figures of mermaids on the balustrade of the palace terrace

Figure of a dancing Bacchus in front of the palace

The palace gallery

Lamps on the palace terrace

The northern side of the palace

Statue of John III (Sobieski)

View of the terrace with the sculpture of Gladiator

View of the northern lake from the palace terrace. In the foreground, one of the sculpted lions, in the background, the bridge with the statue of John III

A northern view of the palace

The Cadet School

The Myślewice Palace

The drawing room on the first floor of the Myślewice Palace

The dining room in the Myślewice Palace

The bathroom in the Myślewice Palace

The ceiling in the bathroom

The drawing room on the first floor of the Myślewice Palace

Sculpture of Chronos and detail of an eighteenth-century French clock in the first-floor gallery of the Myślewice Palace

Picture gallery on the first floor of the Myślewice Palace

The former library on the first floor of the Myślewice Palace

Views of the park

◄ Sculpture of a satyr in
the park

View of the park

A gondola on the lake

A park avenue

The White Cottage

Dining room in the White Cottage

Bedroom in the White Cottage

Chinese Room in the White Cottage

Anteroom on the first
floor of the White Cottage

A neo-classical porcelain
basket dating from the late
eighteenth century

The boudoir in the White
Cottage

Gallery of sculpture and a general view of the Old Orangery

The theatre and the gallery of sculpture in the Old Orangery

Sculpture in the Amphitheatre

View of the park

Views of the park

The Amphitheatre

The theatre café

Sculpture by the Amphitheatre

Sculpted representation of Dawn in the park

The park in the area of the New Orangery

The New Orangery

General view of the New Orangery

The canal in front of the Egyptian Temple

View of the park

The Temple of Sibyl

The Belvedere seen from the garden

View of the park

Bacchante and peacock

The park drive from the south

INTERPRESS PUBLISHERS
Polish Information Agency
ul. Bagatela 12
00-585 Warsaw
Poland

Set by the Polish Information Agency
Printed and bound by
TIZ ZRINSKI d.d., Čakovec, Croatia